The Guitar Music of Spain. *Volume Two.*

Isaac Albéniz (1860-1909)

Isaac Albéniz stands as one of the most significant composers
that Spain has ever produced, influencing future generations by his use
of regional themes and idioms which capture the spirit of Spain.

As a child he was an outstanding pianist, his first public performance
being given at the age of four. Rebellious and adventurous, he set off, alone,
at the age of nine, on a journey which covered Spain, most of the Americas,
England and much of Europe, supporting himself by giving recitals,
returning to Spain after four years.

Deciding to devote less time to performing and more time to composition,
Albéniz went to Paris where he studied with Vincent d'Indy and Paul Dukas,
and was also influenced strongly by Claude Debussy and Gabriel Fauré.

Although his compositions include orchestral music, a number of operas
and songs, it is his works for piano that form the major and most important
part of his output. Some of the piano works require a considerable
virtuosic technique which Albéniz himself possessed (due in part to study
with Franz Liszt), and many are highly descriptive and evocative of the
regions of Spain, the most prominent of these works being Iberia,
Suite Española, Recuerdos De Viaje and the Cantos De España.

This Albéniz collection contains some of the most popular pieces, in
some of the finest transcriptions for the guitar, including three by his friend
Francisco Tárrega, who was the first to transcribe many of the piano works
of both Albéniz and his contemporary, Granados, for guitar. Also included are
some transcriptions by Miguel Llobet, himself a pupil of Tárrega. Both Tárrega
and Llobet did so much in the revival of the guitar and guitar music and
in bringing the music of Albéniz to a wider audience.

Wise Publications/Unión Musical Ediciones S.L.
London/New York/Paris/Sydney/Copenhagen/Madrid

Exclusive Distributors:
Music Sales Limited
8/9 Frith Street,
London W1V 5TZ, England.
Music Sales Pty Limited
120 Rothschild Avenue,
Rosebery, NSW 2018,
Australia.

Order No.AM90241
ISBN 0-7119-3304-9
This book © Copyright 1994 by
Wise Publications/Unión Musical Ediciones S.L.

Compiled and edited by John Zaradin
Original compilation by Gerry Mooney
Music processed by Seton Music Graphics

Cover illustration by Adrian George
Book design by Pearce Marchbank, Studio Twenty
Computer Origination by Adam Hay Editorial Design

Printed in the United Kingdom by
Caligraving Limited, Thetford, Norfolk.

Your Guarantee of Quality
As publishers, we strive to produce every book to the highest commercial standards.
The music has been freshly engraved and the book has been carefully designed
to minimise awkward page turns and to make playing from it a real pleasure.
Particular care has been given to specifying acid-free, neutral-sized paper
made from pulps which have not been elemental chlorine bleached.
This pulp is from farmed sustainable forests and was produced
with special regard for the environment.
Throughout, the printing and binding have been planned to ensure a
sturdy, attractive publication which should give years of enjoyment.
If your copy fails to meet our high standards, please inform us
and we will gladly replace it.

Music Sales' complete catalogue lists thousands of titles and is free from
your local music shop, or direct from Music Sales Limited. Please send
a cheque/postal order for £1.50 for postage to: Music Sales Limited,
Newmarket Road, Bury St. Edmunds, Suffolk IP33 3YB.

Asturias
(Leyenda - Preludio)

By Isaac Albeniz
Guitar Transcription by Luis Maravilla

Allegro ma non troppo

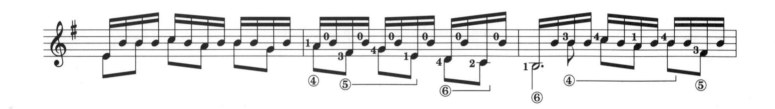

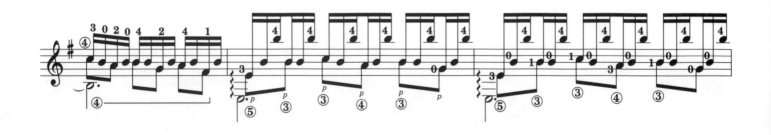

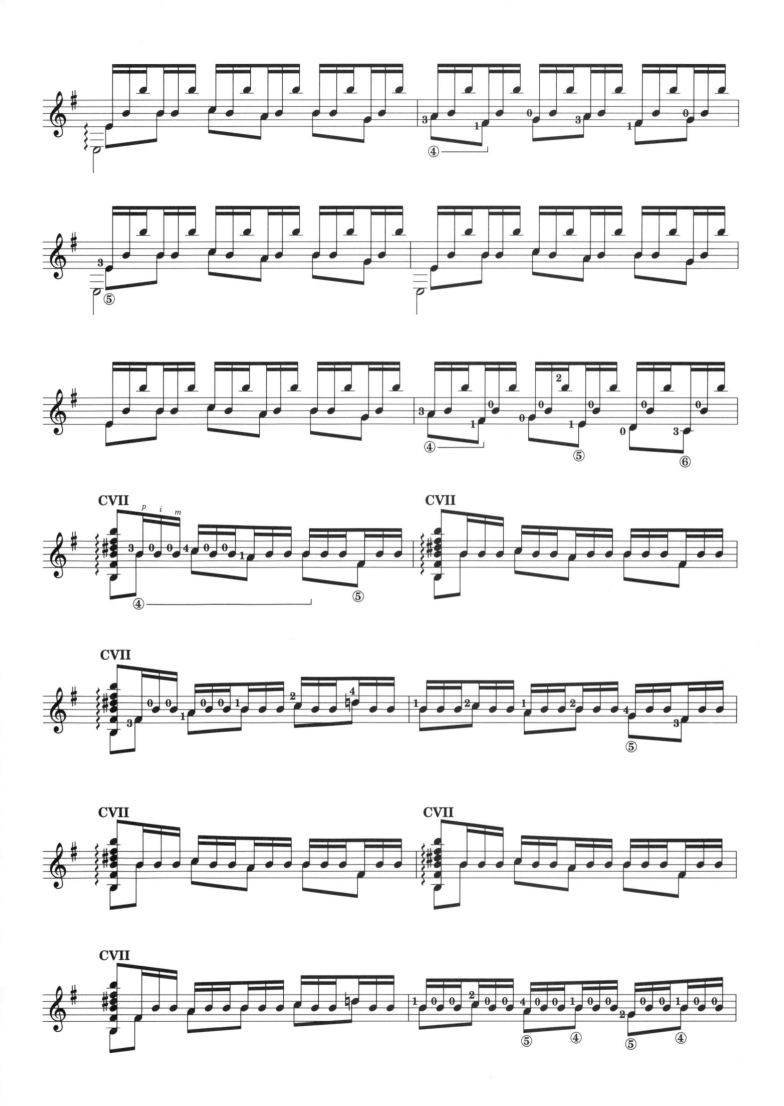

Cadiz
Serenata Española

Music by Isaac Albéniz
Guitar Transcription by F. Tarrega. Revised by Miguel Llobet

Allegretto ma non troppo

Cataluna
Corranda (No.2 De La 'Suite Española')

Music by Isaac Albéniz
Guitar Transcription by V. García Velasco.

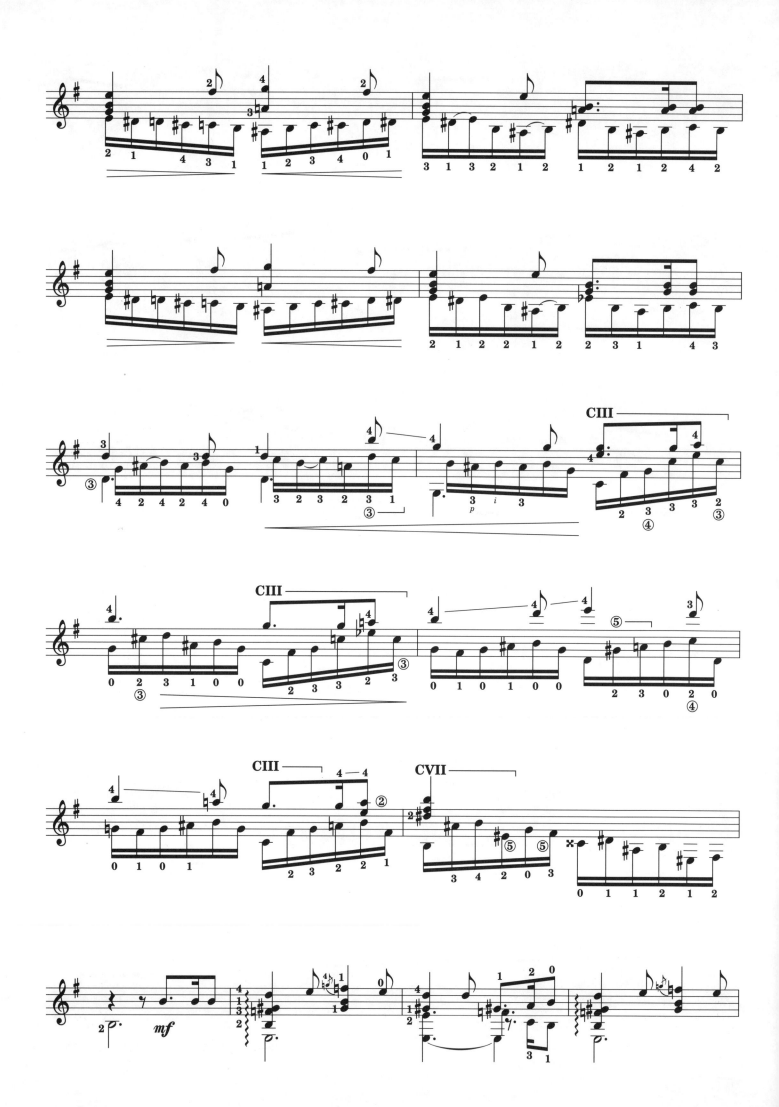

Cordoba
De 'Cantos De España'

Music by Isaac Albéniz
Guitar Transcription by Ernesto Bitetti

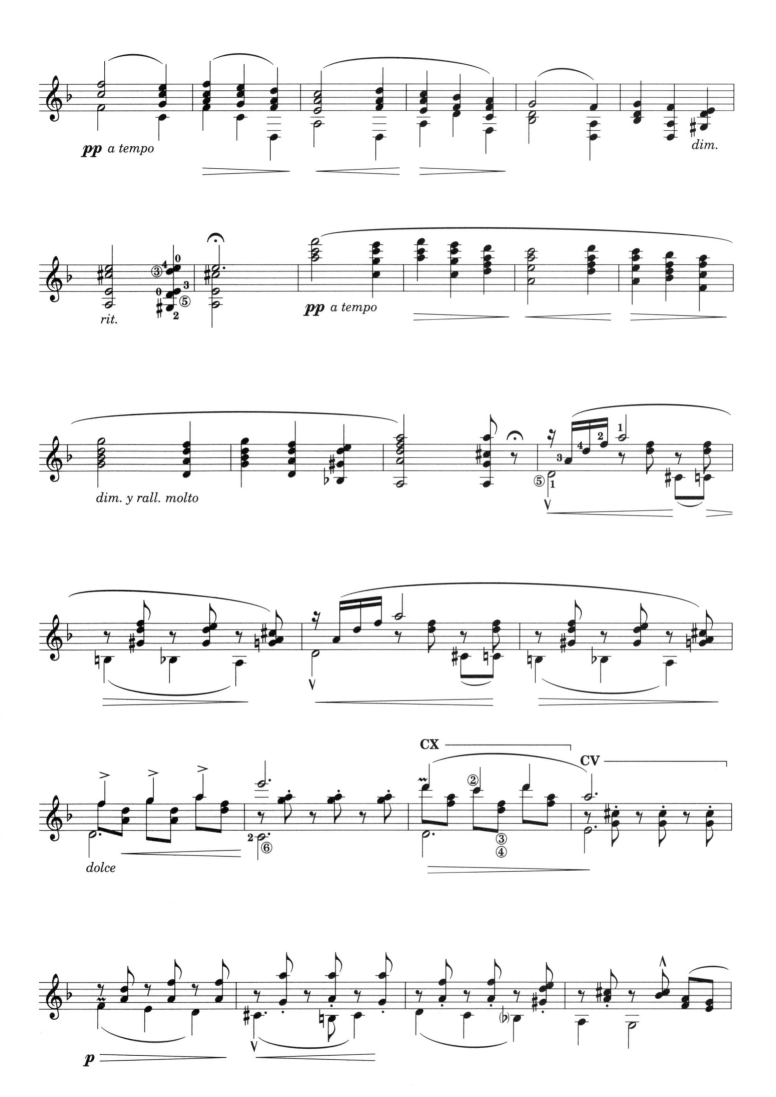

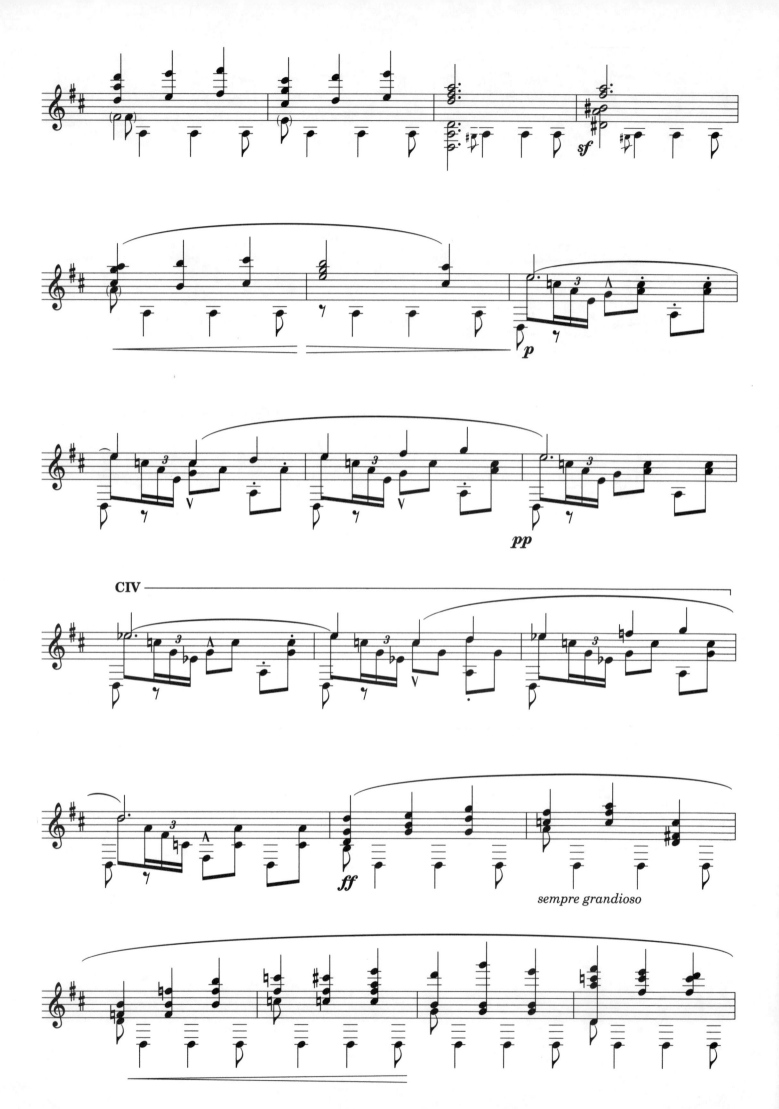

En La Alhambra
Capricho Morisco

Music by Isaac Albéniz
Guitar Transcription by S. García

Allegro non troppo

6 = D   *staccato with the 4th & 5th strings*

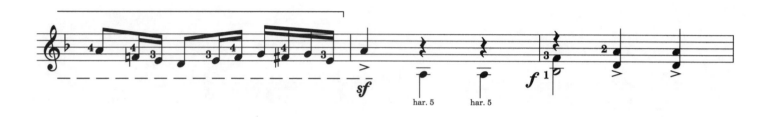

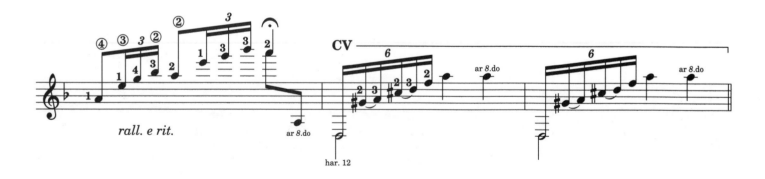

Meno tempo

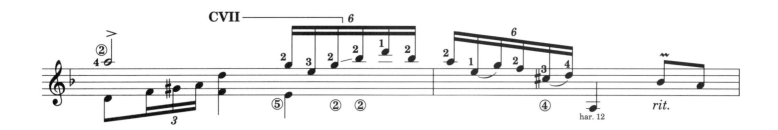

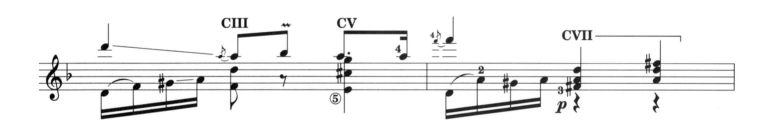

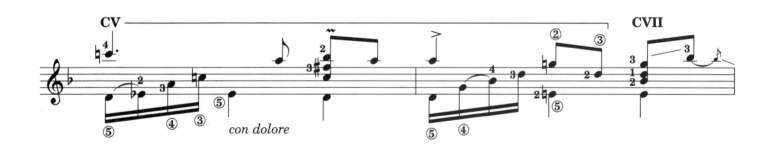

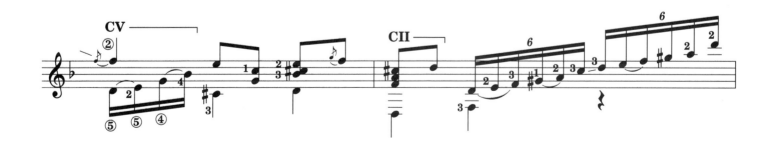

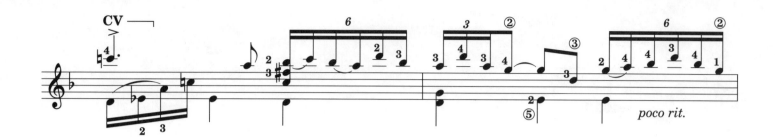

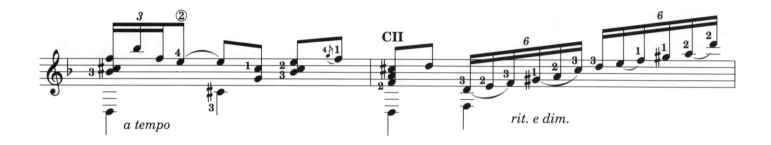

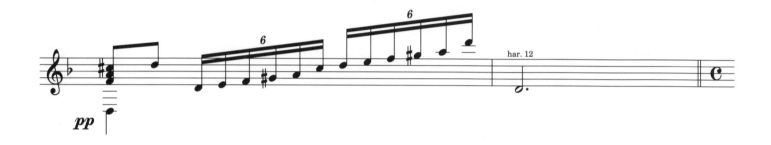

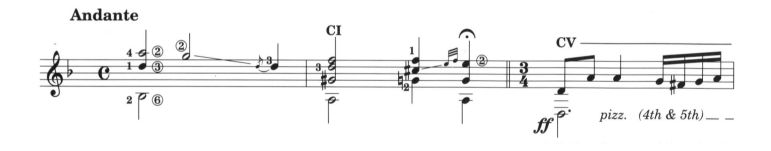

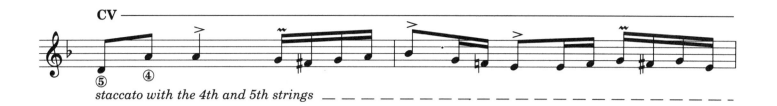

staccato with the 4th and 5th strings

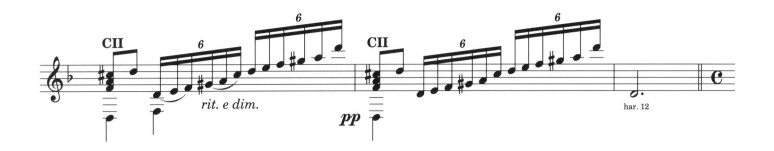

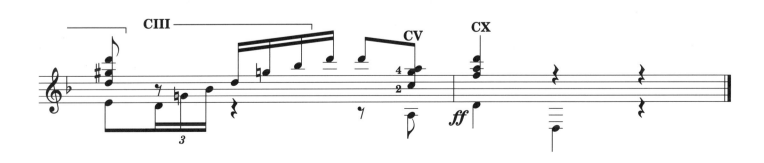

35

Granada
Serenata (De La 'Suite Española')

Music by Isaac Albéniz
Guitar Transcription by F. Tarrega

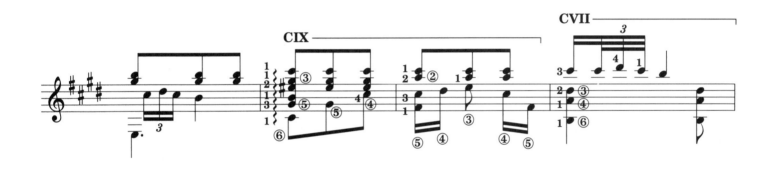

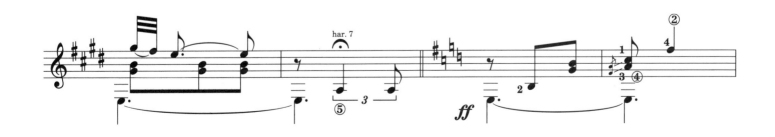

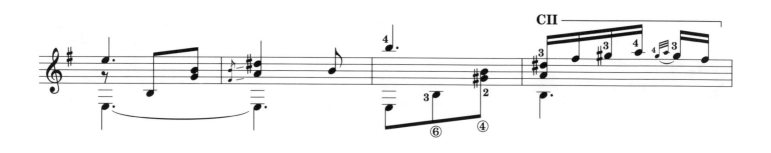

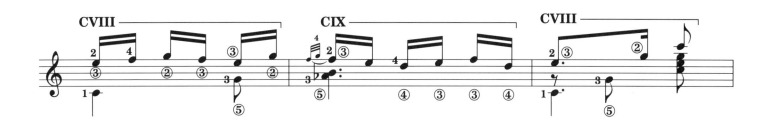

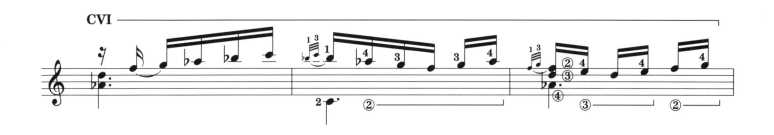

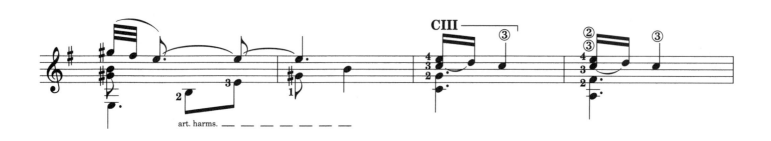

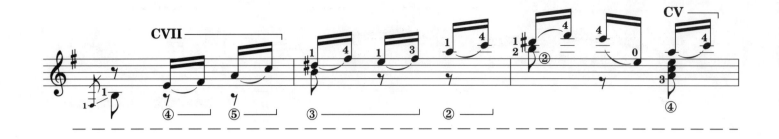

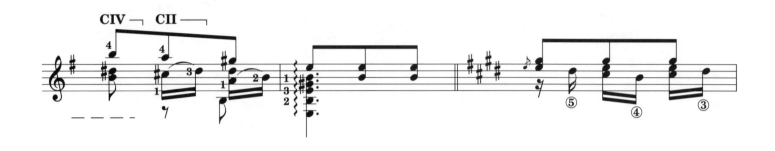

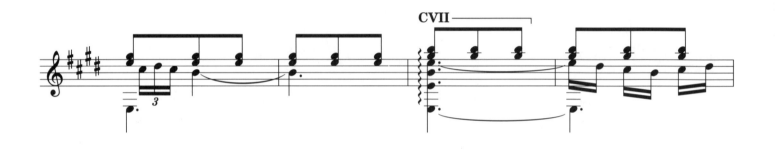

Mallorca
Barcarola

Music by Isaac Albéniz
Guitar Transcription by Luis Maravilla & Luis Lopez Tejera

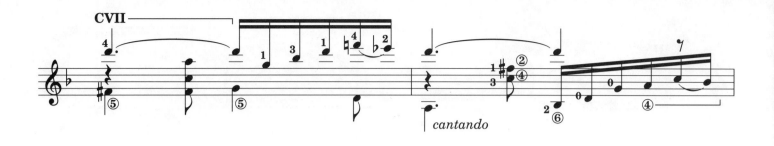

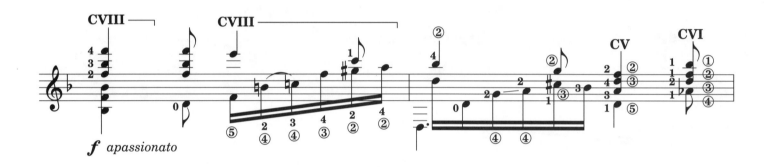

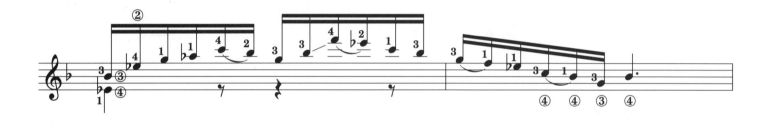

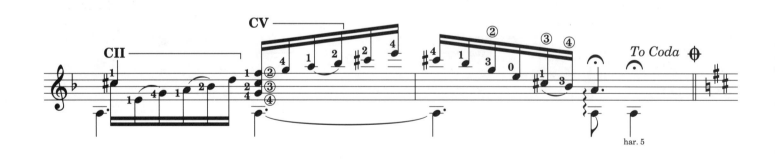

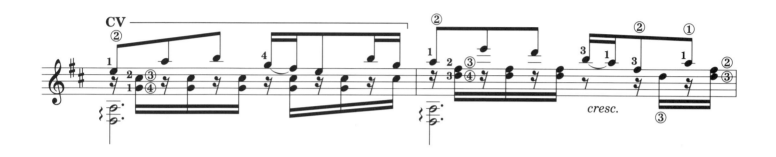

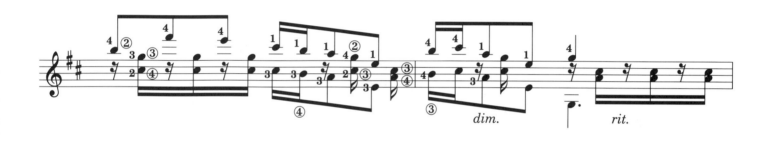

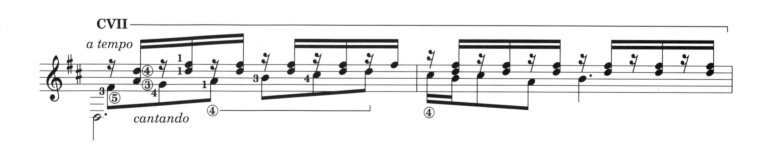

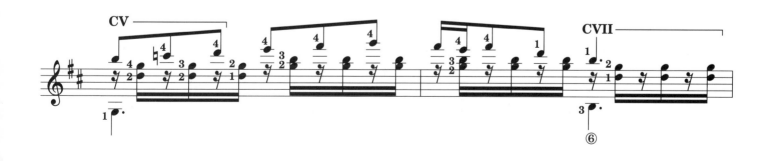

p molto rubato

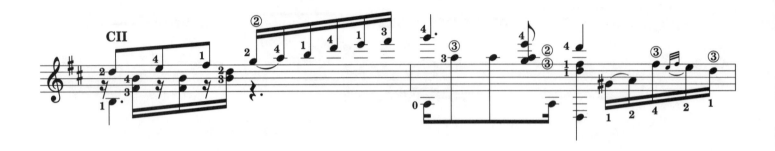

a tempo

cantando e dolce

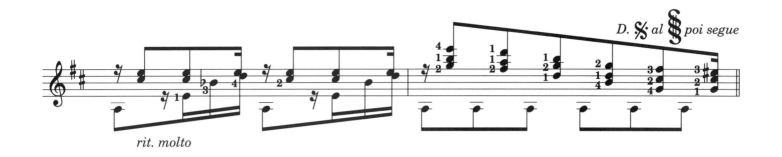

rit. molto

rit. e dim.

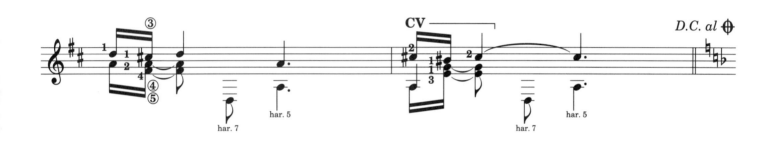

Coda

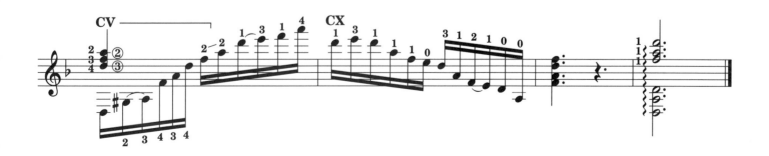

Oriental
(De 'Cantos De España')

Music by Isaac Albéniz
Guitar Transcription by Miguel Llobet

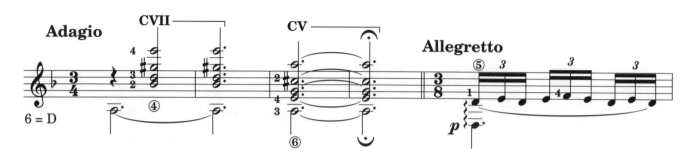

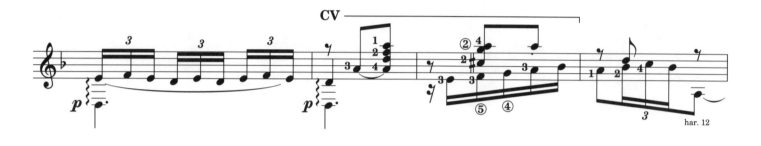

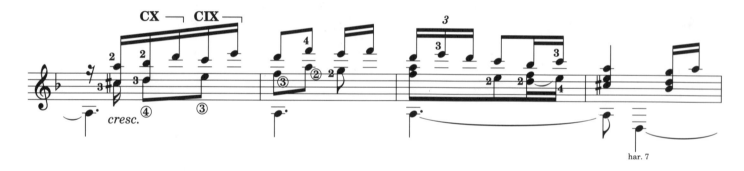

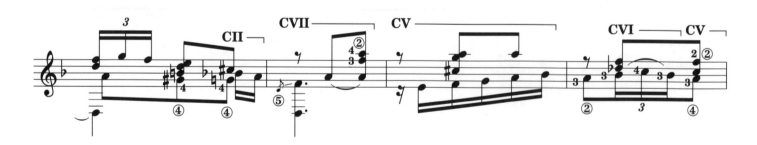

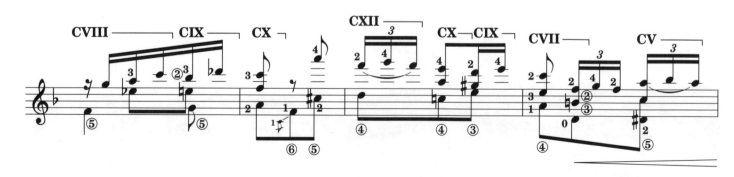

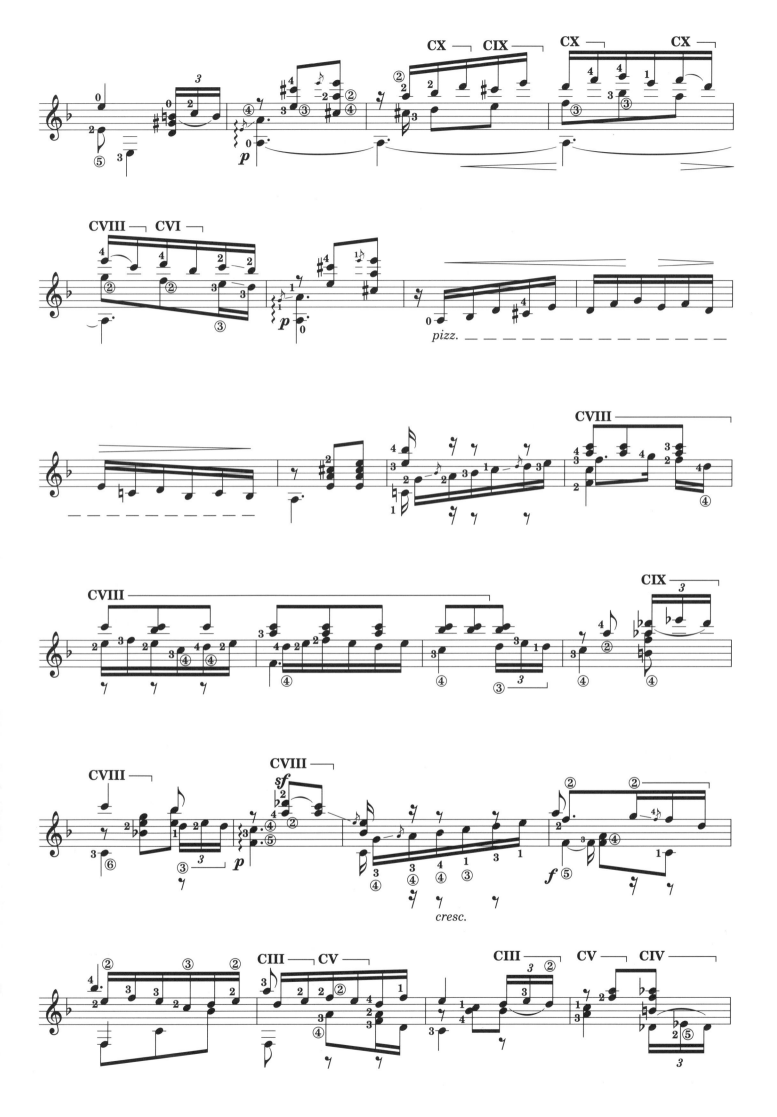

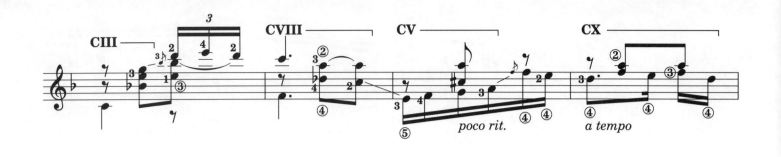

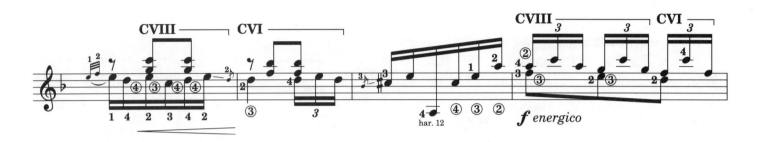

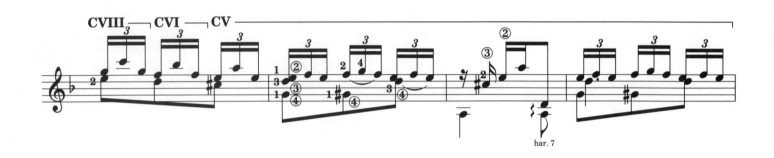

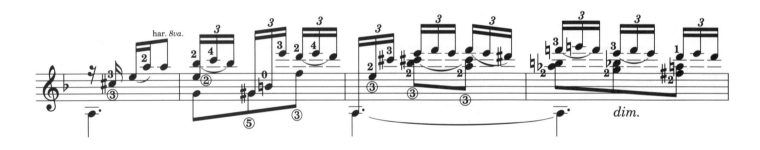

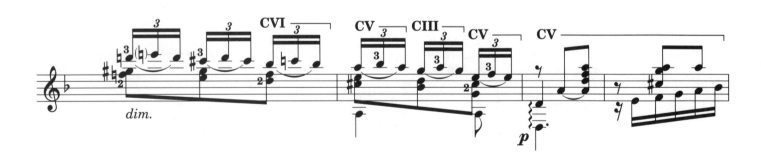

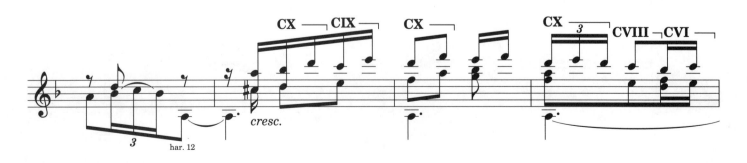

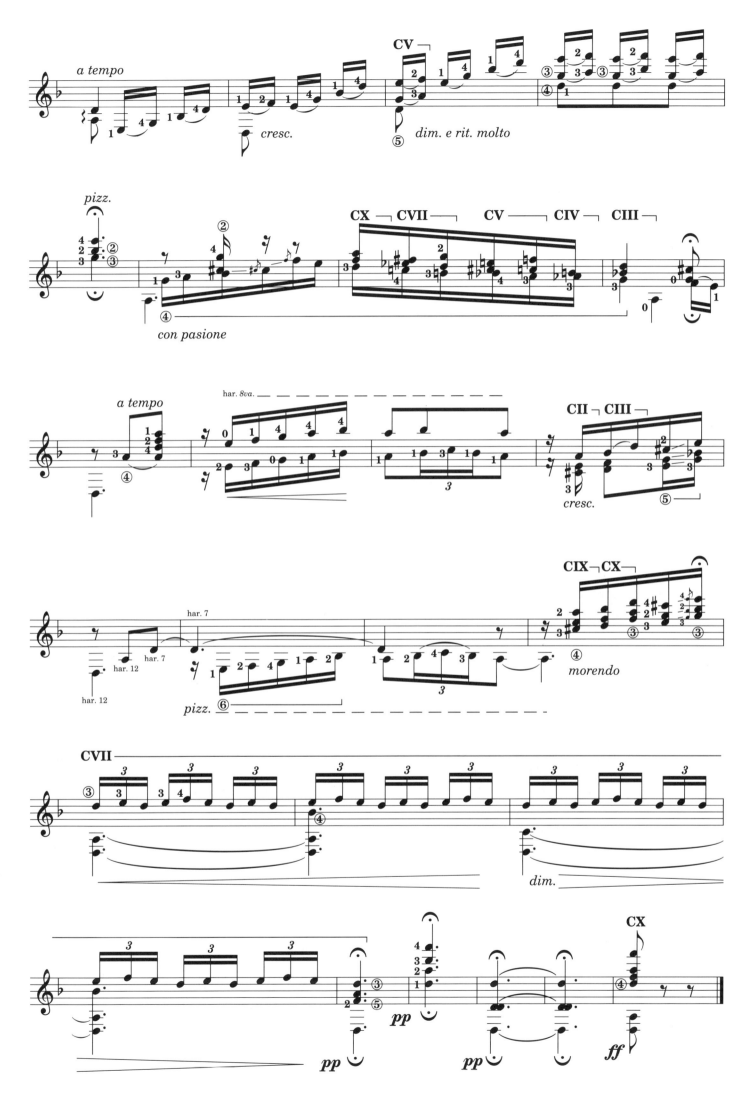

Puerta De Tierra
Bolero

Music by Isaac Albéniz
Guitar Transcription by S. García

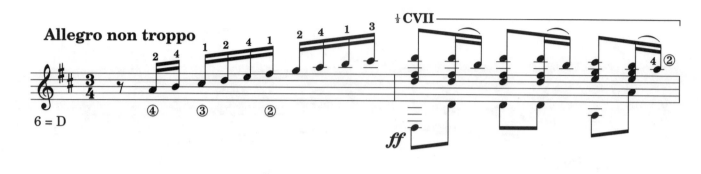

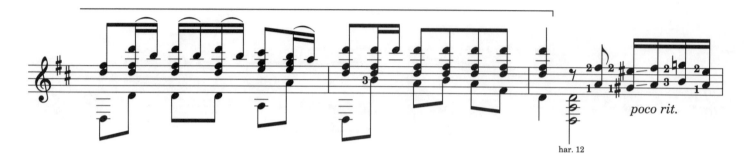

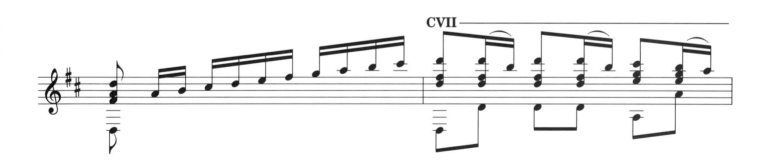

har. 12

Rumores De La Caleta
Malagueña (De 'Recuerdos De Viaje')

Music by Isaac Albéniz
Guitar Transcription by Aureo Herrero

Allegro non molto

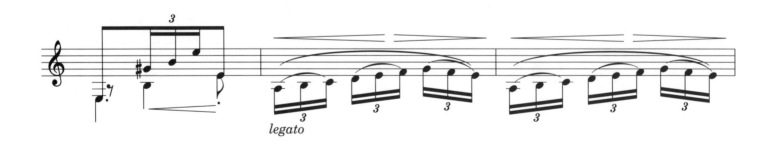

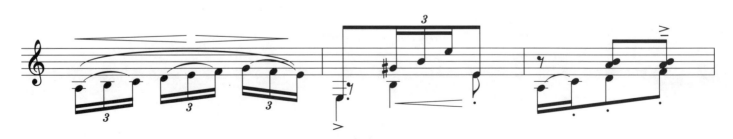

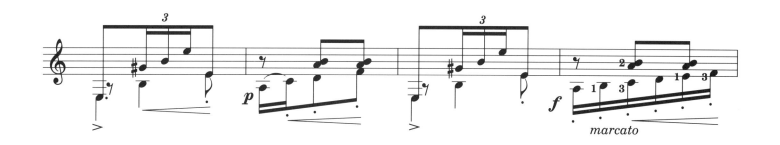

marcato

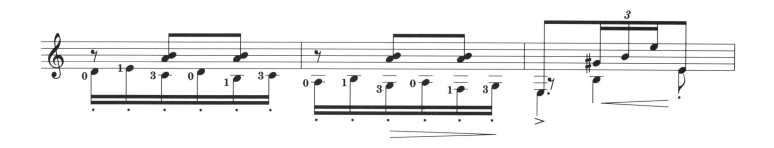

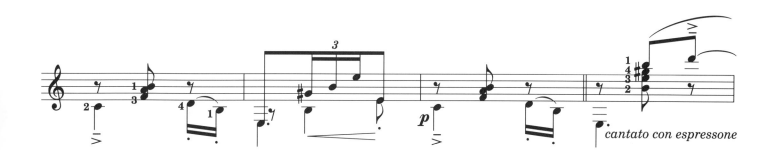

cantato con espressone

poco ten.

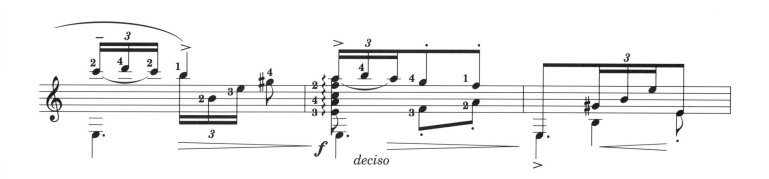

deciso

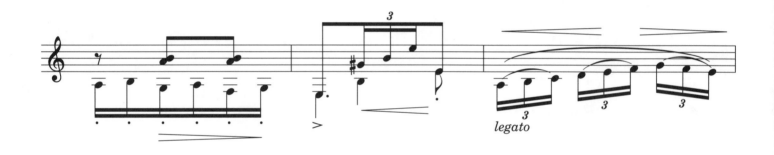

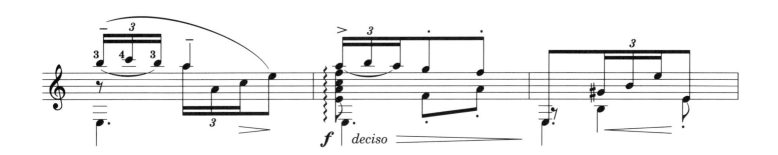

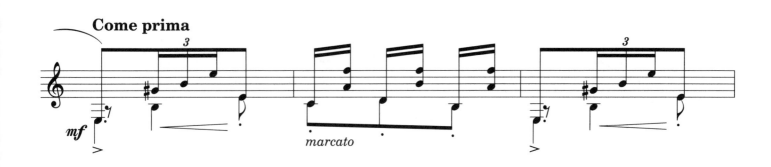

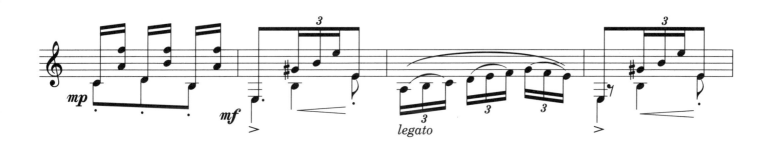

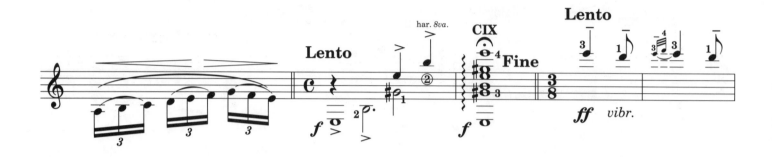

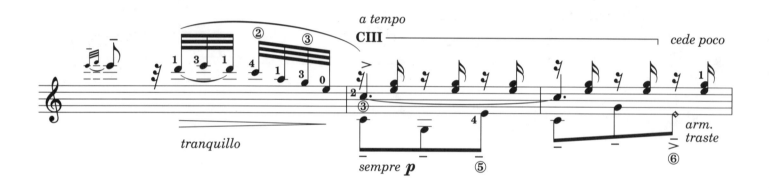

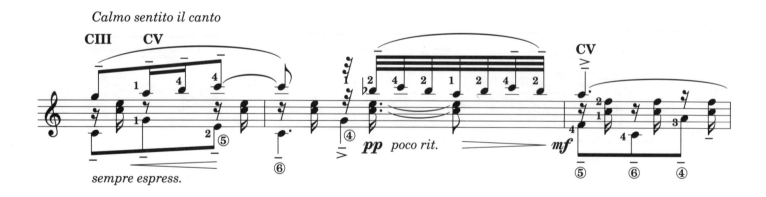

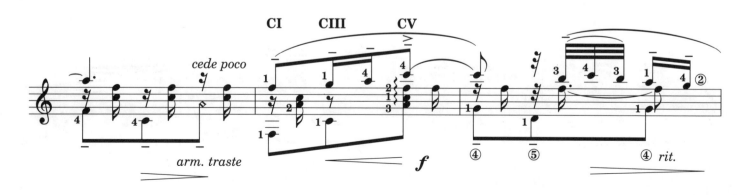

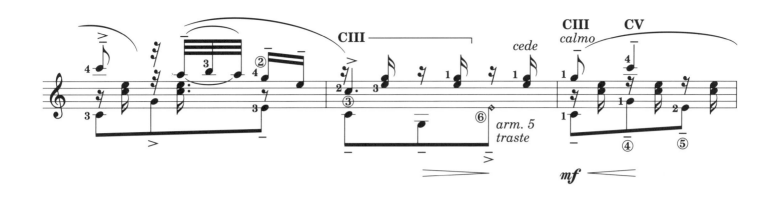

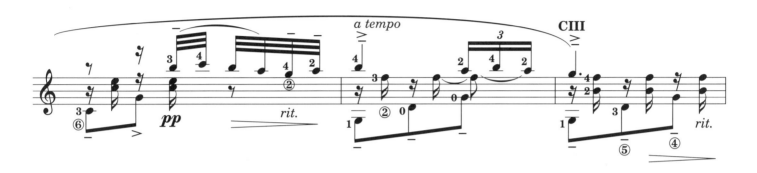

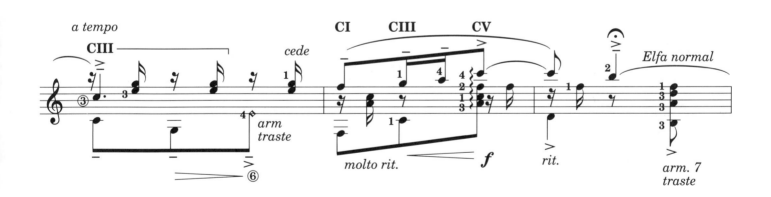

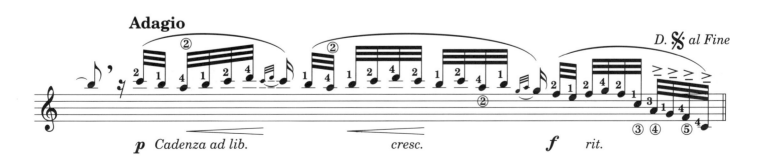

67

Serenata Arabe

Music by Isaac Albéniz
Guitar Transcription by S. García

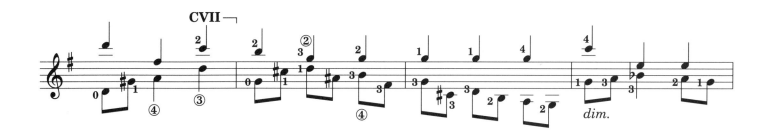

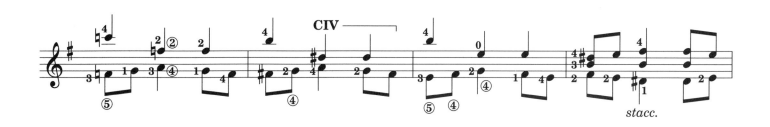

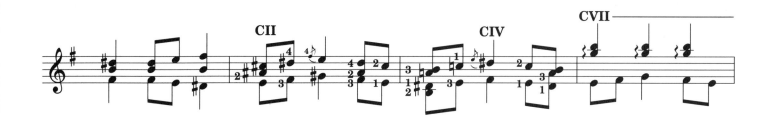

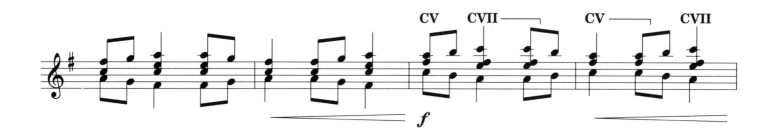

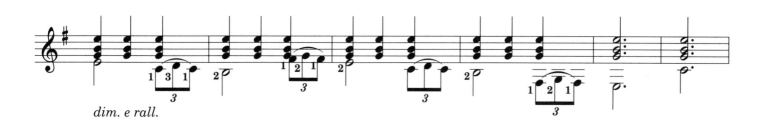

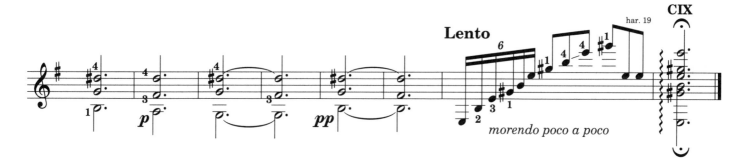

Sevilla
Sevillanas (De La 'Suite Española')

Music by Isaac Albéniz
Guitar Transcription by F. Tarrega. Revised by Miguel Llobet

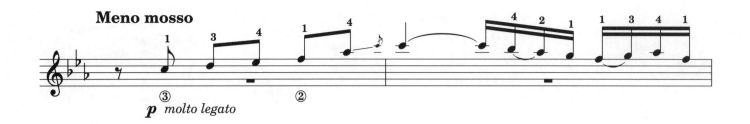

Meno mosso

p *molto legato*

rall. poco

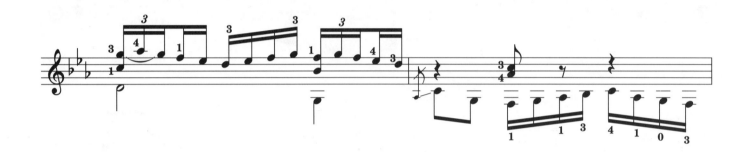

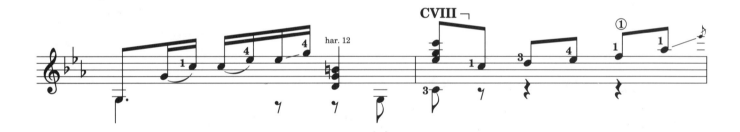

CVIII

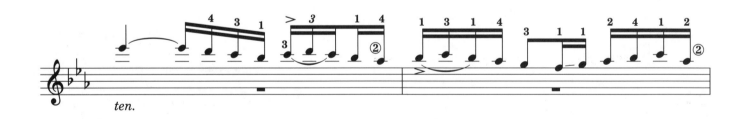

ten.

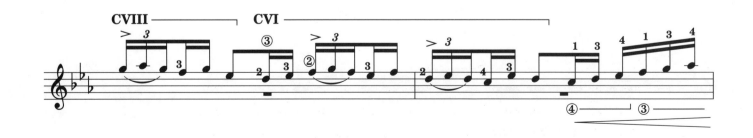

CVIII ——————— CVI ———————

Tango
No.2 De La Suite 'España'

Music by Isaac Albéniz
Guitar Transcription by Venancio García Velasco

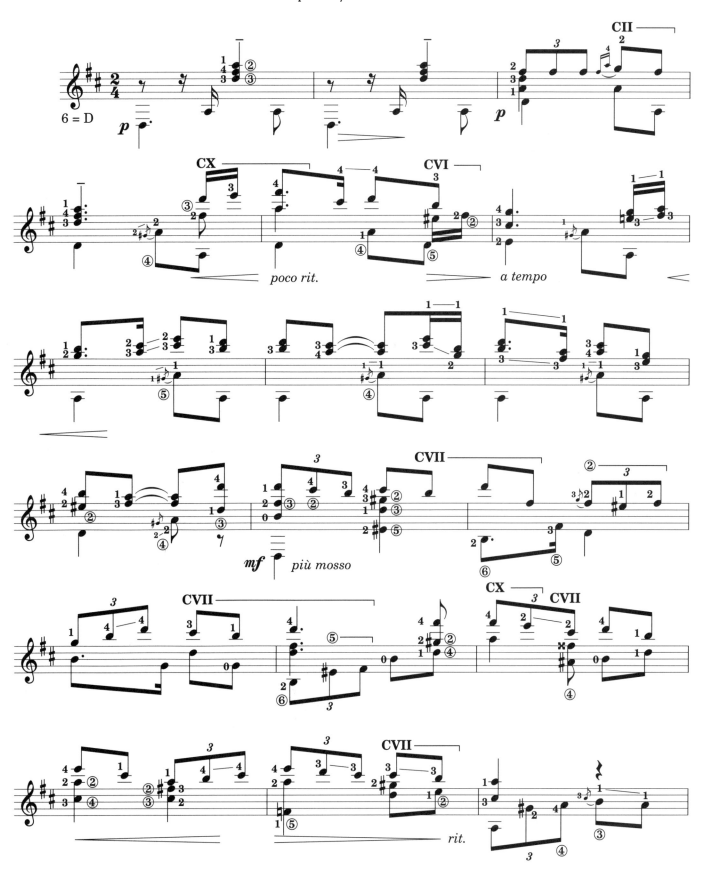

Torre Bermeja
Serenata

Music by Isaac Albéniz
Guitar Transcription by Miguel Llobet